D0547136

White Water, Red Walls

Rafting the Grand Canyon

Poems, Paintings and Photographs by

Carol McMillan

For dear Mr. T, who patiently awaited my return while I was off adventuring. The terror of gophers and mice, he seldom fails to be the warmer of my lap. With his purrs, Mr. T. makes my home a rich and warm abode.

© 2014 by Carol McMillan. All rights reserved

ISBN: 9780990710608

Library of Congress #2014914747

McMillan, Carol 2014. White Water, Red Walls: Rafting the Grand Canyon

Photographs, watercolor paintings and sketches by Carol McMillan
Front cover design by Carol McMillan

Contact author: sylvanease@gmail.com

Photograph by Rebecca Hightower

Contents

Introduction

In June 2014 our group of adventurers rafted 224 miles down the Colorado River. Although many such groups head out each summer, our guides informed us of the seriousness of this journey. Any trip down the river is an expedition, they emphasized to us, not a vacation. As a whitewater addict for most of my adult life, rafting the Grand Canyon ranked high on my bucket list. Still, the Colorado is a river demanding respect. It contains the biggest white water in the United States, using its own ranking system. Not the one-to-six system used elsewhere, Grand Canyon rapids are ranked on a one-to-ten scale. There would be no portages; we would raft the whole river.

At 5:30 a.m. on May 31, 2014, Arizona River Runners picked us up in Las Vegas. A comfortable, air-conditioned bus drove us to Lees Ferry, where we would load our rafts and begin the journey. The bus ride left me plenty of time to contemplate what awaited us. The first two poems, "Anticipation" and "Indifference", were written during the ride.

Anticipation

Still unknown,
the river is running.
Our group has gathered,
our gear is packed,
and the river is running.
Dawn stretches shadows
of yucca, rabbitbrush, and mesquite
long across the sand.
A five-hour bus
filled with strangers
destined for intimacy,
silent except for couples,
each one thinking private thoughts.
One voice of trepidation, with laughter,
"But I have children at home!"
Photos show giant waves
colliding above a raft they dwarf.
The sun is rising.
the land is parched.
Miles ahead,
the river is running.

Indifference

This land
doesn't like humans.
It wasn't made for us.
Water is secreted,
coveted and rare.
So few places to escape the unrelenting sun.
Horned reptiles and tiny rodents
scuttle in shadows,
jealously guarding the their bodies' moisture.
Knee-high forests have thorns and prickers,
defending themselves from all but
the toughest mouths;
nothing here is offered up
luscious.
Yet we come,
we humans,
drawn in a strange way
by the challenge of survival.
We must learn its ways if we wish to stay.
And the soul of this land,
majestic in her indifference,
might speak to us of stars.

Stepping In

The river appears,
wide and green and cold.
Forty-seven degrees, the guides tell us,
while we melt
in a three-digit day.

Our group circles up
in available shade.
Grey rafts aligned,
nosed onto gravel,
looking small.

Forms are signed.
Arizona River Runners will not be responsible
if we should perish.
The atmosphere hangs silently,
more serious
than I expected.

Chris explains procedures.
Fill your water bottles.
Find a number and grab three bags.
Grey rubber dry bags
for bedding and all we've brought.
They'll keep our gear dry
if a raft overturns.

Two weeks completely cut off,
no way to talk with the world outside.
Halfway, there's an eight-mile climb,
the only way out if one chose to leave.
Two hundred and twenty-four miles
on a fifteen foot raft
through America's largest
white water rapids.

With equal parts uncertainty and excitement
I heft my gear
and step in.

Setting Up Camp

Heat and sun and holding on
to a bouncing raft,
diving and crashing through frigid waves.
Each evening "We'll be camping soon"
serve as words of respite for canyon-tired bodies.
Ahead the beach looks tiny in a landscape
that reduces a soaring condor
to dragonfly-size.

Landing, we leave the guides to anchor rafts
tied high above a changeable shoreline.
Stepping or leaping clumsily over long rope lines
we swarm the beach, dispersing at its crest
through scattered tamarisk and random boulders.

Each camper seeks a perfect site,
tradeoffs of how far to lug gear
versus privacy and distance from the snorers.
Or how close to the "Groover"?
Should I set up a tent?
Only a few did – for privacy from rafters and rodents.

Trudging back to shore we line up like a fire brigade,
passing dry-bags, camp chairs,
cooking pots and sleeping pads
hands-to-hands
from rafts to the chosen common area.

Finding three rubber bags with lucky number thirteen
I schlep the lot back to my site.
Hanging wet clothes in thorny branches
I find dry ones, reading glasses, and my journal.
The guides have told us
not to lay out our sleeping bags too soon,
lest we crawl in later to find
adventuresome snakes or scorpions
exploring our beds.
I re-seal my bags before padding back down
to set up chairs in a mutable circle.

Tired bodies trickle in
with beer and books
or wine and words,
choosing a spot or moving some chairs
based on our evening's mood.
Contented, we await the welcome cry,
"Dinner!"

The "Groover"

Legend has it that once there was only
a metal box with ridges
that left dents in ones backside after using.
Hence the name was born.

A box still, but evolved now,
with a regular seat and lid.
The guides place it in a private spot each night,
acceptably distant from camp,
and always with a view.

Early on
I wrote a song,
You Pack in Food and You Pack out S#*t.
Inspired by simple truth, it has many verses.
Each evening
Zach places a row of fairy lights in trees and rocks
to guide our way.

Bighorn

Along the banks
Desert bighorn.
Sandstone-colored sheep
graze and gaze,
surprised by unwieldy conglomerates,
our cumbersome
human-raft forms.
We gaze back, marveling
at their compact utility.

Stopping to Scout

The rafts have been beached
and the guides have climbed high,
Scouting a way down a rapid.
Though the river may flow one hundred feet wide
they search out a very thin path.
A rock on the right, a strong eddy left,
each raft must thread its way through.
There a great "keeper hole" lies along the left bank
while a standing wave looms just below.

Hydraulic jumps can result in a hole
in the water that's fifteen feet deep!
We'd be spun round and round
like a washing machine
conjured up in a maniac's dream.

Our oarsmen decide on a serpentine path
that they've scratched out and mapped in the sand.
Just the width of one raft,
it snakes a way down
between obstacles seen from above.
But once on the water
memorized moves are required
to carry us through
when the white foam is flying,
the passengers screaming,
and large rocks are looming too near.
When eddies reach out to swing back an oar,
while a hole tries to suck us straight in.

Our guides scramble down,
satisfied with their map;
they know they can paddle us through.
They've done it so often,
though every time's new,
their confidence steadies our nerves.

The rafts launch from shore,
And we're off…

Canyon Morning

"Hah-ot cof-feee!"
The cry goes out
after indigo has turned to grey.
From my sleeping pad
I stretch and yawn,
slowly rolling up and off my bag,
too hot to have slept under covers.

Acknowledging the fading stars
I pad down the beach
to fill my ARR cup with dark brew
and nod a grunted greeting.
We sink randomly onto the chairs
of last night's circle.

As if being careful
not to startle us awake,
the morning sun
gently lowers itself
down canyon walls,
turning greys
to ancient reds and golds,
peacefully welcoming us to this canyon's
seventy millionth new beginning.

Watercolor by Carol McMillan

Red Wall Cavern

A tiny mouth-slit
at the base of Red Wall limestone
grows as we approach
and grows
and grows
into Red Wall Cavern.
Our guides say football fields
could fit inside.

Toward the back I find
traces of once-living creatures
now crushed beneath a mile of stone.
Someday
we may also be
smudges of color
somewhat interesting
to something sentient.

Tributary

Through the dark Tapeats Formation
sacred stone mines itself.
Liquid turquoise
flowing on travertine,
confounding with its beauty
any long-held beliefs
concerning the color of streams.

Fifteen miles upstream
it springs full-blown from the Earth.
"The Sipapu" speak the Hopi,
the place where humans climbed
from second world to third,
carrying with them two instructions,
Always respect one another
and sing in harmony
from the tops of all the hills.

"The Little Colorado" say the colonizers,
"Simply a tributary."

I lie down
to let turquoise wrap my body.
A sacred honor.

Bathing

That evening we asked the brothers
to abandon their camp for a bit.
Shallow bays offered rare bathing places;
these men's tents bordered a good one.
Despite their protests of sexism
we women claimed the space,
passing Johnson's Baby Shampoo as freely
as we shared laughter.
We dipped and squealed
in the Colorado's liquid ice.
Later, using nail scissors,
Ginger gave me a grand
Canyon haircut.

Phantom Ranch

After six days camping with rafts,
halfway down the river,
an oasis with cold beer,
souvenir T-shirts,
phone service,
sinks and real toilets.

Intrepid humans hiking the canyon
thought we rafters brave.
Some of us mailed postcards
stamped to tell recipients
their mail had been carried out
on mule-back.

Ethan gathered us up,
herding somewhat reluctant feet
back to the rafts.

At Phantom Ranch half of our group hiked out of the canyon. Their places on the rafts were filled by twelve new people who had hiked down from the rim to join us.

To Those Hiking In

Eight miles
boots and sand
down through layers band by band.
Eight miles
of canyon sun, thirst and heat
before you're done.
Eight miles
you must hike down
to meet the group, but look around;
the red-dyed limestone, Muav shale,
and Red Wall all have tales to tell.

Ancient creatures lived on Earth,
swam in seas
and all gave birth to ancestors
now so far past we'd never claim them,
but they last
in sandy layers pressed and formed
by massive forces
to take forms of fossils
we can touch and know
compressed a billion years ago.

But keep on stepping
down the path of dusty boots
and reach the rafts where unknown friends
await with warmth to bring you
to the group we've formed.

"Crystal Rapid is one of the most feared and
respected rapids on the entire Colorado River."
Arizona State University

Crystal Rapid

We rafted down the jewels today,
the boats all pulled to shore;
even after many days
this run requires more
considered consultation.
For Crystal our guides paused,
they pointed, looked, they talked and frowned,
they knew that Crystal was
the rapid with the most respect,
the one that harmed a guide,
the one whose consequence has made
the oar folks to decide
to run it left
or run it right.
They didn't all agree.
Each chose their own and rode the tongues,
we had to wait to see.

Translucent green rose high above our heads
as we flowed in,
but turned to froth of crashing white
to make us flip or spin.
Our guides held true their chosen routes,
they brought us safely down.
ABC, Alive Below Crystal!
Pass the beer around!

Tracks

Lizard and mouse tracks,
Each nocturnal wandering
Etched in silt-fine sand.

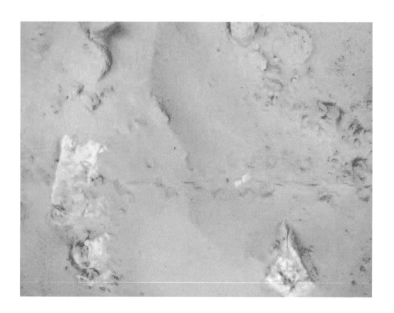

Shinumo

Shadowed slot
A thin canyon paved
with ankle-twisting cobbles.
Clear pools hold endangered
Humpback Chub.
Ethan's joy in finding them to show us.
With a small stick he gently herds them out.

Collared Lizard Courtship

Huddled in a bit of shade
we hang out
while others hike.
Just a small sandstone overhang,
barely shade for two.

But soon a third,
A collared lizard scuttling across the sand
just behind us.
And then two more.
The first chases the second
and both want the third,
undoubtedly a super-sexy,
hot mama lizard!

Dashes and passes,
approaches and fleeings,
chases and turns.
Playing coy with two suitors.
Then one.
Then touch.
He hops on and hops off
and they are done.

Not much can be said
in support
of collared lizard sex.

Photograph by Rebecca Hightower

Canyon Play

Echoing liquid and laughter,
a side canyon
surprises with joy.

Tongue of the Rapid

Flowing green glass depths
Blanketing the rock below.
Our raft glides over.

"You really don't want to go left at Bedrock."
Rafting Grand Canyon

"Crystal and Bedrock are two rapids to not make
a mistake in." *PaddleOn.net*

"One afternoon at a rapid known as Bedrock, the
Bright Angel was sucked into an immense chunk
of granite that splits the river in two, and its
entire side panel was raked off,"
Kevin Fedarko, *The Emerald Mile*

Left Down Bedrock

A "chick day" on our raft.
joking and laughing and being bawdy.
Shoshanna rowing us down through rapids.
She was awesome yesterday
in her perfection through Crystal,
a scarier rapid than we'll face today.
Ahead lies Bedrock,
a mass that splits the waves.

"Stay right", they say at lunch.
"Stay right", the guides all say
after we hike the Black Tail trail.
In shadows of the towering cliffs
Ethan reads aloud
stories told of other's lives.
But back at shore
we laugh and joke,
"No tail till after Black Tail."

"Stay right," the guides had said.
We all load up.
The rafts swing out.
We watch each disappear.
The river's horizon,
they drop below,
swirling up and crashing down.
We watch them ride the waves.

"Stay right!" White foam.
They all stayed right.
Now we glide down
the glassy tongue.
A circle of waves bending right,
but some pour left
around that monster rock.
Shoshanna pulls.
She pulls some more.
Her oars churn
through the river's strength.
And there it is, the massive rock,
seeming much too close.
And then we hit,
but not too hard. Maybe, still . . .
we could go right.
Powerful water
pulls us back, going left.
"Go right," they all had said.

"Get down!"
"Hold on!" "Oh shit!"
Shoshanna yells,

frantic with one oar to pull.
We spin around,
go through a hole,
then slam again
against the rock.
"High side, High side!"
Shoshanna's voice
to make us right the raft.
Ginger climbs the upward side
risen much too high.
While Becky leans behind to grasp at
Kristy swimming hard,
Somehow thrown out she's right below.
She'd been up front
but now behind,
how has she gotten there?
And I reach too.
Just inches gape
between our hands
but Kristy drops below my sight.
The water sucks her down.

Then slammed again,
we meet the rock.
Sideways,
fast against hard stone
the raft is held,
left side down with right side up.
Arms out-stretched to hold two straps,
I'm crucified against the raft,
holding on with all my strength.
The water roars against my chest.

There's screaming just beyond my ear,
I turn my head to see.
Sandwiched on the face of rock
the raft I'm in
holds Ginger's body pinned
just feet away.
Shoshanna linking Ginger's eyes,
"Push up, Push up!" She yells.
And Ginger pushes,
Ginger screams.
A ton or more of raft and waves,
are pressing out her life.
Fantastic power
in arms and legs,
Ginger fights the raft.

I cannot move,
I cannot help--
the water holds me fast.
With hopelessness I watch
as Ginger fights for breath.
Suddenly
the raft breaks loose
and swirls a turn,
now Ginger swims below,
beside the raft and in the waves.
I'm reaching out to pull her in,
she stretches far to reach me my hand,
and then, again,
the rock is near.
We pull apart

just in time.
Another crash of raft and rock.
Again it turns.
The current grabs.
A devil's dance.
Waves crashing down.
The raft is whipped on through.
Frigid water fills the boat,
and then the river calms…

On my knees,
at least chest deep,
I look around.
No one is there…
Shoshanna, Becky,
Ginger, Kristy,
all have been thrown out?
Where are they now?
And how are they?
Sick inside, I do not know.

"Bail," I think, to get control
"bail" to raise me up.
"Bail," the only word I hear
though none is there to speak.
"Bail." Are other rapids near?
The pile of gear a mountain
to be scaled to reach the oars,
but there's no power in my arms.
"Bail," I think, or this won't steer.
Who knows what lies ahead?
Bail to reach the oars.

I'm floating on,
and then ahead
Jacob's raft comes near.
"Please catch me,"
all I whisper out.
"We will," he answers back.
"Don't let me pass."
"I've got you,"
as he's giving Paul his oars.
Jacob jumps
and clears the gap, now safely in my raft.
"Stop bailing, Carol."
I bail some more.
"Stop bailing, Carol," again,
more firmness than before,
"Come to the mat."
The raft's stern is a frigid pool,
I think he grabs my vest.
Jacob pulls as I climb up.
"Are you OK?"he asks.
"I'm fine," I say,
but shake too hard to stand.
More questions that I can't recall.
I somehow pass his test.

He rows ashore,
some golden sand,
heaven glows ahead.
Someone from another raft
reaches for my boat.
Jacob grabs a rescue line,
he leaps onto the beach.

Running now,
he seeks to save the others
from the waves.

Trembling hard,
I climb ashore.
I want to hug the sand.
Sunshine, friends, and chocolate bars
are welcome treatments,
easing hypothermia.

Another raft
rows up behind,
then sodden Shoshanna's here.
We fall into each other's arms
to hug and sob and sooth.
Two are safe, three still unknown.
We hold each other tight.

A cry goes up!
We look across,
Kristy has appeared.
Atop Bedrock
she stands and waves
to signal she's OK.
Self-rescued,
she has climbed the rock,
now waiting for a guide
to eddy back and reach the rock
to bring her down to us.

Across the waves,
beyond belief,
Ginger stands on shore.
Although I'd thought
I'd watched her crushed,
she signals she is fine.
I hope she is
but don't feel sure.

Four of us accounted for,
but Becky still unknown.
Ten minutes last for ten more years,
no one knows her fate.
"She's passed us by?"
I ask the group.
"No," a few reply.
"We all have watched; we would have seen."
I wish I could believe.
But if not there, then where? I think..
Caught down beneath a rock?
The minutes keep on ticking by
and we all hold our breaths.

Another cry,
across the waves,
and Becky, too, is found,
also clinging to the rock
below where Kristy stands.
Jason and Jimmy row to them;
the two guides bring them down.

We later learn that Becky's feet
had slid beneath the gear.
Pinned there
as her side went down,
she'd found herself submerged.
Her feet slid free
she loosed her grip,
but the water pulled her down,
then let her up,
but down again,
she thought it was the end.
Resigned to fate
her body limp,
pulled both cold and deep,
but then the river spit her out.
Desperately she gasped for breath
and reached to hold the rock.
Amazingly, with random grace,
the river let her go.

All the rafts now reconvened;
our group has made it through.
No more waves
of mammoth size
will challenge us this day.

Stay right, stay right at Bedrock,
'Stay right,' the guides all said.
But we went left at Bedrock
and none of us is dead.

Watercolor by Carol McMillan

Sounds of a Full Moon

The whisper of sand
with a breeze past my body,
a vision of silence
that murmurs aloud.
The flutter of bat wings
a black lace mantilla,
the roar of the river
a muffling shroud.

The curve of the limestone
a mile high above me,
blushed by the moonlight
to show itself red.
The colors of layers
awakened in nightglow
beckon my spirit
to slide from my bed,
to sip from the stillness
and taste constellations
collected below
in the indigo sky
that lies in the water
to float down the river,
to dance on the waves
as I watch them slip by.

The sun of the day
that has blistered my body
caresses me now as he
shines from the moon.
Liquid and languid the
velvets of shadows
lie soft on the sand
but will lighten too soon.

Bonded

I've never been to war and hope I never will.
It seems an awful thing,
having learned to hate or kill.
Yet soldiers let civilians know
there's nothing like the bond
of knowing someone has your back
if ever you are wronged
or in a place where you could die
without the help of those
who'll risk their lives to keep you safe,
you'll be the one he chose
to stand beside, to share her strength,
there's nothing like the bond
that grows between the ones who know
they'll keep each other strong.

But now I have a sense of it.
The enemy we faced
was not one of the mortal kind
nor of the human race.
Both love and fear we hold for her,
the canyon we came down.
Her dangers taught my core to know
that caring can surround
a group of strangers
come to hold each other's lives so dear.
We found we'd gladly risk our own
despite the weight of fear.

I found a place inside myself I never knew was there;
A place to help another live rose stronger than my care
to keep myself alive and well.
Our instincts made us reach
without a hesitation
or the thought that we might breach
a pact of self-survival we thought we might have made
but found instead we'd leave it if another could be saved.
As others risked their lives for mine
I found that human souls
are not the greedy, selfish things
we often have been told.
Without a thought, a human offers all to help a friend
who finds herself in danger.
I've found that, in the end,
it's not about our unique selves we wish to keep alive.
We're pieces of a larger web of instincts to survive.
I wish that soldiers never learned
this lesson with such pain.
I wish that everyone
could learn it gently and remain
more innocent. I'm grateful for
this awesome canyon's gift.
I hope I'll know it always
and allow this thought to lift
my spirits when I feel alone
or when depressed or blue:
I'm bonded with a group of friends
who helped each other through
the beauty and the terror
held within the sandstone walls.

Our guides have done this many times,
to them the burden falls
of making sure we all live on
to love another day.
I know they've given me a gift I never can repay.

The river roars, the canyon
holds these lessons for the ones
who dare to venture down,
then live to greet another sun.

Photograph by Arizona River Runners Guide

Canyon Time

Time is a complex concept.
Hours and seconds
exist only in our minds,
mere concepts from our culture,
no basis in reality.
With no clock to mark their passing
they cease to be.

Days, however, reflect a reality,
marking the rotation of our planet.
But I choose not to count them
while we're on the river.
Time fades and flows,
an eternal now,
until that "now"
becomes the day we have to leave.

Photograph by Rebecca Hightower

Climbing Out

On our final day
a pre-dawn float ends at Diamond Creek.
The rafts are unloaded, deflated, and trailered.
Hugs, promises, and even some tears.
After weeks as protectors the guides depart,
returning to Flagstaff in air-conditioned comfort,
while we clamber onto an ancient white bus.

Our Hualapi driver bounces and careens us
up graded dirt and tumbled rocks.
Sometimes a creek bed, winding and climbing,
this "road" does not submit docilely
to use by a vehicle..
The driver's seat swings freely on springs,
protecting his body from rattled disintegration.

Laughter and groans,
lurches and bashes.
On the battered old bus thats dashboard is dusty,
I note with concern a warning light blazing.
But our driver ignores
a screaming alarm sounding shrilly
above all the grinding and clanking.

Eventually, stopped with a last final wheeze,
the bus delivers us topside
to the rim we've scarcely glimpsed for weeks.
With icy Pepsi and salty chips
we re-enter a world once-familiar.

Photograph by Rebecca Hightower

It was a shorter ride back to Las Vegas than our outbound journey had been, but it still left plenty of time to contemplate the world we were about to re-join.

Silencing Its Voice: Southern Nevada

There's a culture of benders and breakers
who take the land
and twist its soul.
With wetland ancestry they've come,
ripping and digging
and paving and damming,
running lines to bring in coolness
and carry their voices.
They light the night to hide the stars.
Golf courses and mock pyramids
where there should be
Joshua trees and desert tortoises.

Go home, intruders.
Go home to your places of fog and mist.
Leave this land to those who adapted,
who studied its nature
and learned its ways.
Leave this land to the ones
who hear its voices.

The Gift

Do you know the smell of red sandstone
baked too dry for touch?
Do you know the smell of the river,
cold in its greenness?
Do you recall the feel of sand
shifting softly underfoot?
Can you hear the song of a canyon wren
complaining of chewy food?

Do you remember the place where
clock-time wasn't and
moon-time was?
Where water sang lullabies while
you watched infinity in the stars?
Despite cars and coffee,
clocks and deadlines,
you still hold knowledge of that place.
Turning inside,
at any moment you can
ride a mind-rail downward,
sliding into a spot of
secret peace,
the canyon's lifelong gift.

Acknowledgements

Gratitude flows through me in colorful waves, gentler than some of the waves of the river, but no smaller. Massive thanks must go to those who kept me alive through the canyon, thus making a reality of a long-held dream and the resulting poems, photos, and paintings that have become this book. The Arizona River Runner guides fed us, saw to our physical and, when appropriate, mental health while rowing us down the mighty Colorado. At times, when the mercury was bursting out the tops of thermometers, they rowed us through "quiet water" against powerful headwinds. At other times, when the water turned wide and white and wild, they found a narrow path of current and wound us safely between rocks, "holes", and giant eddies that would easily flip our rafts. When an incident did happen, as the powerful, always changing river occasionally insures, the team worked together as one to bring everyone safely through. The phrase "they held our lives on their oars" was in a poem that I didn't include here, but I must honor our guides with the truth of those words. Chris Louderback, Jacob Sack, Jimmy Hendrick, Julie Clinton, Ethan Johnson, Shoshanna Sack, Zach Fitzgerald, and Jason Mackelprang, I tip my battered sunhat to you all.

I also wish to thank those who have believed in and encouraged me as a poet. A camp counselor once asked for a copy of a poem entitled "A Wind-swept Pine Tree" that I wrote as a Girl Scout in the Sierra Nevada mountains. "Cricket" said she wanted to keep it for when I was famous. What excellent words of encouragement to give a 12-year-old! I also owe a debt of gratitude to Alice Dammen and Thelma Achamire, two dear friends who always encouraged my writing. Sandy Vaughn in the Okanogan Highlands of eastern Washington was the first to convince me to read at coffee houses, and C.J. Prince introduced me to the poetry community of Bellingham, convincing both them and me that I had something to contribute. And, finally, I wish to thank my courageous editor, Andrew Shattuck McBride, who was the first to make suggestions to improve my poems. One writes poems from the soul, so making adjustments to them seems scarier than making adjustments to more academic writings. Thank you, Andy, this is now a better book as a result of your suggestions.

I shall be forever grateful to these and others who have supported me and encouraged my pen to keep moving as the grateful slave to my unpredictable muse.

Carol McMillan
Bellinghan, WA
October 16, 2014

53

CPSIA information can be obtained at www.ICGtesting.com
Printed in the USA
BVIW12n0907090115
382596BV00001B/1